About the Author

Narissa Minta Gavu was born into a devout Christian family, where her unwavering love for God was nurtured. Her life unfolded as a journey deeply rooted in faith, compassion, and a relentless pursuit of inspiring others. She found solace in reading and writing as hobbies in her early years, which formed the foundation of her interest in writing.

Narissa's professional life has been solely dedicated to the health sector, where she has spent considerable years serving humanity as a professional nurse. A career path much of a calling, a test of faith, compassion, empathy, and above all, love for others.

Narissa's vision is to inspire and uplift people from all walks of life. Her poems are vessels of hope, encouragement, and spiritual nourishment. She aims to touch hearts and rekindle a flame of positivity through her poems.

HIDDEN IN THOUGHT

NARISSA MINTA GAVU

HIDDEN IN THOUGHT

Olympia Publishers
London

www.olympiapublishers.com
OLYMPIA PAPERBACK EDITION

Copyright © NARISSA MINTA GAVU 2024

The right of NARISSA MINTA GAVU to be identified as author of this work has been asserted in accordance with sections 77 and 78 of the Copyright, Designs and Patents Act 1988.

All Rights Reserved

No reproduction, copy or transmission of this publication may be made without written permission. No paragraph of this publication may be reproduced, copied or transmitted save with the written permission of the publisher, or in accordance with the provisions of the Copyright Act 1956 (as amended).

Any person who commits any unauthorized act in relation to this publication may be liable to criminal prosecution and civil claims for damage.

A CIP catalogue record for this title is available from the British Library.

ISBN: 978-1-80439-171-6

This is a work of fiction.
Names, characters, places and incidents originate from the writer's imagination. Any resemblance to actual persons, living or dead, is purely coincidental.

First Published in 2024

Olympia Publishers
Tallis House
2 Tallis Street
London
EC4Y 0AB

Printed in Great Britain

Dedication

An inspiration for all.

Acknowledgments

May Almighty God receive all the praise and glory for the gift of life, and wisdom for the thought to write this book to inspire everyone and generations yet to come.
To God be the glory!

INTRODUCTION

Hidden in thought is an inspiration and a console for young and old.
The book is structured into two sections.
The first is solely inspiration, and the second part is a console of words (poems you may call it).
Many of us go through stressors of the day which may be unexplainable.
You may not be the first,
I may not be the last; but inspirations serve to calm our nerves and console our hearts.
These and many reasons inspired the writing of this book, enjoy my piece!

A NEW BEGINNING

New beginnings are necessary
You might feel crowded now
Or caged wishing for freedom
Everything might seem out of reach

Do not feel rejected
You are not alone
A rolling stone gathers no moss
And none of us is neither a stone

We need people around us
A circle of people who care
To live with and interact
Life is meaningful with the right people

Years have gone by
You've met many people
Young and old
And various personalities

Somewhere along the line
Some people remained in contact
Others just disappeared from our lives
These are all part of human nature

New beginnings should be part of us to:
Mend broken hearts
Restore relationships
Bring lost smiles on our faces

A new beginning
A new behaviour
A new self esteem
A new world for us all!

WORDS OF THE HOLY SPIRIT

Have you wondered why I am so into you?
Have you ever thought of my intention?
Becoming your friend is just a plus

Remember my friendship is not for fun
I want to draw you closer to The Father
I never forgot your words of 'thank you' for favours received

Be mindful that the road is not smooth at all
When you fall, I go down with you
And you will rise again and again

I will never stop knocking on your door
Until you come to terms with your calling
The Lord is your strength

I am The Holy Spirit
I am the spark of your conscience
I am the silent speaker

SUNDAY

Sundays may seem to be normal days
Usually, it is a day of less activity worldwide
Little do we know it was designed for all goodness

Sundays are not just ordinary days
Scripture relates it as a day of rest
The day God rested after creation

Offices are generally closed on this day
And most people are off from busy schedules
But Christians depict Sundays with church service

In fact, Sundays are days of total serenity
There is a kind of stillness in the atmosphere
Days we all have the best sleep no matter the time

Sundays should be days of rest and reflection
Unfortunately, rest is not part of some people's lives
The human body needs a break and rest once a while.

MY TRUE TASK

My true task
Your true task
Something vital

This should be a conversation
Wish you were here for the meeting
My seats are empty, I'm still waiting

Let us begin with a prayer
The heavens are far, but near
Say Amen to answered prayer

As you plan, ideas flow like stream
As you plan, strive achieving them
As you plan, keep hoping

When you fall, be up standing
Until all is swallowed, keep drinking
The race is still ongoing

Careers very important to some
Families most precious confider of others
Relationships taking the best of us

As you continue to satisfy your desires
Proving to the world how good you are
Think of your Maker and how to do His will.

GOD'S PROMISES

The promises of God are true
God created his children with lots of gifts
From our looks to our abilities are all part of his blessings
Bible made many references to inform us of His love for us
His promises are the evidence of His love for us which we long to enjoy

God's love is supposed to bring joy, make peace and console hearts
However, this rather warrant envy instead of admiration, create
foes instead of a team
The difficulties we encounter in our lives are not
His will for us
Overcoming trials build our faith in Christ

If you have the eyes to see all the promises of God for us
You will then know the depth of his love for His children
God promised Canaan to the Israelites
But He did not reveal the challenges ahead

With gifts untold He has in store for us
The promises of God are everlasting
They shall not return to Him void
His promises are true and Amen!

MIRACLES SIGNS AND WONDERS

It is difficult to believe in the supernatural
Miracles, signs and wonders can be imaginary
We have many religions and diverse beliefs
But some beliefs are common to all

Miracles, signs and wonders do exist
Even though they do not happen often
These are evident in the Holy Book
Believe to experience the supernatural

This is not about higher thinking nor the sixth sense
Let's say when all you needed was a solution to a problem
When all possible avenues for help has been exhausted
You must be conscious of your needs when you're expecting a miracle

Until you trust and try it
Miracles, signs, and wonders have a specialty in saving the day
These bring impossible results when you least expect it
In whatever form, expect yours today!

THE POWER OF YOUTH

Can you recall any moment in your early years?
Aside your childhood where you just eat and play
Remember crawling or falling asleep?
Do you recall any decision you made?

Youth to me is breaking from a shell
A shell full of energy
A shell filled with enthusiasm
A confinement with such endurance

The joy of youth is natural
Guided by the supernatural
It remains everlasting
And worth reminiscing

Engage your parents in a conversation
Ask of their best moments
Do not be surprised of the outcome
They usually begin to beam with smiles

They will either be lost in the moment
Stare at the ceiling or smile at the sky
In a moment, your presence will not be felt
As they are caught enjoying the beauty of the past

Your best looks is in your youth
Most love stories begin at youth
A stage most lifetime decisions are made
A ground of getting the puzzles right

A phase to discover yourself
Appreciate who you are
This is the power of youth
Where life begins.

AN EXCELLENT POTTER HE IS

Now admiring my eyelashes
As one just fell from its pore
The curve and its finesse

An excellent potter he is
To fix the lashes in curves
Away from hurting the eye balls

The eyes very powerful
So inviting as it sparkles
Expressing pleasure and pain

An excellent potter he is
This I say to myself, and all agree
Anytime I look in the mirror

I try to look beyond
How attracted I am to hairs
No wonder it's all over me

Massage your scalp
Touch your cheeks
Your armpit, oh! Do not go there

An excellent potter he is
Have you thought of your make-up?
I mean your natural self

They are well arranged
Yes, they are fearful, can scare someone
Yet, so wonderful and very useful

An excellent potter he is
His creativity is just amazing
Thank you for making me come true.

A KNOCK AT THE DOOR

A knock at the door
It's midnight
Someone knocks at your door
What would you do?

Would you respond?
"Yes who is there?"
You just hear someone mumble
Is it enough evidence to open up?

What is your name?
You just can't make a meaning from the murmur
Now there's silence
Would you open?

Compare the time and your life at that moment.
Very dicey, huh?
Sieve your thoughts
And make the right decision

Have you got any emergency contact?
Do you have concerned neighbours who look out for you?
If you cannot open up at that hour of the night
Then you cannot open up to any stranger

It is important to be useful
But be useful at the right time
Your safety should be your priority
Think through, it will help

Be careful of lions
Always ready to devour
Take no chances with life
It is worth living.

THE WISE STILL LEARNS

Wisdom is a gift from God
It's great to be wise
The wisdom of man is his strength
The wise always think through before acting

Wisdom is rare
Believe in the gift of the wise
The counsel of the wise surpasses all
That I will continue to grow in wisdom

However, this does not deprive me:
From failing
From falling
From fighting
Because the wise still learns

As a wise man
When you fail, strive to succeed
When you fall, help yourself up
Continue fighting till you win

This gift opens doors
That's the weight it carries
Remind yourself of the wisdom you possess
And make good use of it.

MY LIFE

My life
My health
My being

My family
My friends
My love so dear

Doctors are no determinants of life
Nor the true sustainers of health
My existence is still in God's hands

I wish you knew my true self
The purpose for my existence
It all remains with the supernatural

Family know you are okay
Friends know you are filled with joy
But the truth is on a journey

Dusk and dawn
Midnight and noon
All make day and night

Some stuck with deceit
My love should know best
All remains with me.

MYSELF

One of the first essays we studied as pupils was 'Myself'
This is simply writing about your personality
And further on adding your likes and dislikes

Every writer draws inspiration from various sources
Even in their lows they still put words together
This makes each piece unique and diverse

Cast your mind to when you first wrote about yourself
How simple was that as compared to writing about someone?
What about the length of time it took to create a vague story?

You know yourself better than anyone
Which is why you easily scribble essays about yourself
A genuine character needs confirmation from no one

Life would have been much easier if we were all good people
But sadly, not in this world I must say
Fate plays its role by presenting us with second chance, yet most fail

It must be a dreadful task to choose to be a villain
Always having to plot and scheme against others
Change for the better and write a good story about yourself

GOODBYE SORROW

I'm a dreamer
And still dreaming
This is my lifestyle

In my sleep
In broad daylight
It's still the same

Goodbye sorrow
Goodbye fine arrow
It was such a blow

Thought you were part of life
So I paved the way for you to walk in
You had a seat and made yourself comfortable

Unlike the tongue with taste buds
You walk with a tint worsening situation
Oh! how cruel you are

I have really tolerated your existence
You cannot get the best of me no more
At last, I love myself

Thanks for the lessons
Charge me and I will foot my bill
And a receipt for evidence of your power

What a degree I attained
None will endure your torture
Who will give you that space to exist

I have reached my threshold
There is a measure of you
But this can't be experienced for the other

Goodbye sorrow
Goodbye fine arrow
Had I known

Go, go, go away
Every human deserves happiness
Go, go, go away
Never visit ever again!

TRUE LOVE

Where are the Romeos and Juliets?
Are there no Cinderellas and Princes?
Is true love far from reach?

Questions remain unanswered
My thought is choked
I'm gloomy and shattered

Fingers remain crossed
Doors kept closed
Everything seem vague

Heartbeat increases
Longs for a console
For security

A heart opened for companionship
Opened for fulfilment
For true love

Love your heart
Find its match
True love does exist

MEMORIES

Lost in thoughts
Missing a lot
My childhood alas

A great stage that fades
My sound nights I miss
Mum's soft kind kisses

Lost in thoughts
Close to reality
Something is missing

Songs from mum
Games with bro
Meals from sis

Cherished moments
Family love
Fun to reminisce

I miss my guard
My protection
My safety

No boundaries
No locks
Afraid of beasts

Lost in thought
Hope to be found
Great memories remain

MY HEART MY PET

My heart my pet
My heart my secret
My heart my solace

Your presence I don't miss
Your shape is such a wonder
Simple in sight yet very delicate
Silent yet your communication travels abroad

My heart finds solace in trusted few
Rejoices with those who rejoice with her
Life is short brew them like beer
The fewer the merrier

My heart my solace
Your signals are complex to explain
Continues to flow like rain
My happy moments and pain

My dream my heartbeat
Don't generate palpitations
If emotions could move mountains
Then mountains could've moved nations

My heart my pet
My bed my console
Don't ever get hurt
Just be calm and remain my pet

MY OWN

Let's link
Let's think
No time to blink

Time to work it out
Use expertise handout
Sell out and cash out

Have to acquire all I aspire
Get all I admire
An owner than to hire

My patience is slow
Bringing me low
Losing all I know

My own makes me responsible
Show all I'm legible
With that I'm comfortable

Fight for your own
Stand on your own
And be in control

RIVER OF LIFE

This river
Such water
Flows forever

Ever delighting
More quenching
Always relieving

Paves the way
Carries impurities away
Banks feel reluctant to pay

Cleansing from within
Nourishing everything
Bringing the best in the least thing

My pain
Your gain
Anything else is vain

This is the river of life
Where I came forth
It is the cycle of life

TOGETHER AS ONE

My legs are too weak to walk
Like a mountain you are to me
It's my wish to climb to the peak
To see what you are made of
And have the experience of reaching the skies

My hands are always swinging about
Searching for a helping hand
Like a shadow you are to me
I wish you will come alive
To be able to reach you in time of need

My palms are extremely soft
Fragile like a day-old baby's
Like a tree of thorns you are to me
It's impossible to hold you in my hands
To feel the connection between us

My skin is extremely sensitive
Like a sharp edge you are to me
It's difficult to come close to you
Even though I need a warm embrace
When I try out of curiosity I will bleed

I'm sweet scented
Inviting like the queen of the night
Such fragrance will blossom our world
But you a strong fume you are to me
Choking me to stupor

The world comprises of givers and takers
The sun shines on the earth
It is in giving that we receive
Let's make a difference
Together as one.

MY GREATEST FEAR

My greatest fear
Seems to be near
More than my dear

It's a vague feeling
Thoughts still ringing
Heartbeats remain pounding

As though I'm daydreaming
Probably it's my imagination
The ball still rolling

I wish this never was
let me go into the subconscious
Something so precious

My greatest fear
The thing is clear
There's no space to come near.

SCARS

Scars are growths we hate to have on our skin
It feels weird no matter its nature and this lowers our self esteem
Formation of scars is a symbol of healing

People spend time and money to cover up their scars
The reason is we are shy of people seeing them
Others may also get to know we've had bad moments

Grace your scars with confidence
There is nothing like healing
And nothing like overcoming a breakdown

Why will one cover scars?
Truth is healing doesn't come with the pain
Your scars should rather be a symbol of strength

Roses are beautiful yet full of thorns
Reach out to plug one and have your finger bleed
That should not stop you from embracing this unique plant

It's impossible to go through life without being broken
I'm yet to meet a perfect human
Embrace your scars.

SLEEP

Sleep is our remote control
You cannot be strong forever
The greatest fighter was even defeated

This is something eyes cannot see
Yet its weight is incomparable
It lingers until you surrender

Sleep comes slowly as though seducing you
It lures you with its charm until you're drowned
This is one thing that defeats every Tom, Dick and Harry

When you're not even ready to give in
Sleep drowns you in its pool
When it calls, you must obey

No matter your status
It gets to make all succumb
This is the power of sleep

TEARS

My tears
My fears
Crystal clear

They are narrow
Filled with sorrow
From a bow and an arrow

These tears
Why not enter my ears
For no eye to see

These tears
Throughout these years
Choose to run down my cheeks

These tears
Leave dry tear marks on my face
Making its traces visible

Slowly these tears
Run into my mouth
To quench my thirst

These tears
None can borrow
Soothing the sorrow

SILENCE IS GOLDEN

Silence is golden
Precious like a token
And not for the broken

I grew up playing with words
Teasing people was worse
Until I found myself in a mess

Have you wondered why people gossip?
Don't be amazed if you are next on the list
Let them enjoy the puzzle and your tips

Silence can be frustrating
Keeps you deliberating
You're either idle or thinking

Silence calms situations
Shares no conversation
Engages no celebration

Silence generates peace
Mine improved my wellbeing
Yours should mould your personality

Silence is still as water
Sounds like a whisper
Weighing the thoughts of a writer

HAPPY BIRTHDAY

Birthdays are happy days
Shivers down your spine all day
Make the best out of your day

Birthdays bring happiness
Great tunes from legends
Tasty meals from best chefs

Unless I discover your favourite scent
I cannot get you any perfume
You might not like it

Unless I get to know your size
I cannot buy you any wearables
It might not fit

Until I get rich
I cannot buy you the world
Am not yet up to the task

There is only one gift that is everlasting
That is our friendship
It always blooms and assuring

Happy Birthday!

DREAMS

Dreams, dreams, dreams
We all have dreams
Some fulfilled, others pending
And those that will never be

Dreams are not just the supernatural
They are not experienced when asleep
Neither does it pertain to visions
Nor a collection of drama

Dreams should be part of your life
It makes you proactive
And helps in planning
You should work toward your dreams

Nobody plans to end up in failure
However, don't give up when it happens
Learn from it and move on
Strive and do better next time

It feels fulfilling to have all your dreams in reality
Do not force dreams when they delay
Do not struggle to reach the finish line
No stumbling block is greater than your dreams

Submit your dreams to God
Back it up with prayers
And hope for good results
Strive till you win.

ALL IS NOT LOST

Genuine spirits
Fair souls
Calm hearts
Love birds

In my opinion
Sincerity speaks for itself
Sacrifice is an aspect of love
Respect is its morals

Love with purpose
Distance is no barrier
Each day draws you closer
Make right all wrongs

It hurts when love departs
Love should not disappear
Matched hearts must stay together
Love should always be home

Do not go away
Wish I had a way
For love to stay
And cuddle all day

Rest in my arms
Feel my heartbeat for the last time
Your memories will linger
Your love remains

THE DESTINATION

Growth is inevitable
Nothing should stop you from growing
You age as the days go by
You grow in knowledge and learn from experiences

You are full of possibilities
Know that you can do all things
Believe in yourself
And work hard

Destructors are many
Do not give up anyway
You are the author of your story
Choose your roles wisely

Do not give up
Should you be discouraged
Remember why you began
And do not be overly expectant

Nature is beautiful
Embrace it
Remain in your lane
You will get to your destination

BEAUTY

Beauty is a state of the mind
Left for me I don't mind
Unless to remind
Someone else to decide

There is no befitting word
That connects like a cord
More than smiles abroad
On a face so broad

My name is beautiful
I'm always cheerful
Everything about me is wonderful
Everyone knows I'm adorable

My definition of beauty
To adore a pretty
Just because I'm her buddy
Is surely ticked than her daddy

There are shades of beauty
I'm not an idle beauty
You're neither the definition of beauty
This makes us beautiful

A thing of beauty is not mighty
As ugly is not dirty
There's no definition of beauty
We're all unique in various ways

LOVE

Matters of the heart are delicate
It's my wish to begin well
And hope to grow in love

If love could be felt
I imagine it to be extremely soft
And its taste very sweet

Love can be sensed miles away
It sounds as it appears
Its charm I always admire

Love is no race
It is natural
Advances with years

Love is pleasing to the eyes
Itches your ears
Keeping you with smiles

Love sooths your soul
Making you whole
Thinking you have it all

I'll say love is unexplainable
She feels it's complicated
He thinks it's all adventure

Love brings pleasure
Without the painful part in play
Love is not complete

IMAGINE A BLIND

Just imagine yourself blind
You don't get to see the beauties around you
The faces of voices who console you
And those who care for you

Friends who join in tears cannot be judged
Fellas with encouraging gestures can't be seen
It'll be heartbreaking when you cannot identify loved ones
And those who despise you when they're right beside you

The most painful part of this I'm sure is
You don't even get to see how charming you look
Not to mention the wonderful parts of God's creation you
possess
You can only imagine

Anytime you meet a blind
Extend a helping hand to them
They need it and will appreciate your kindness
They are waiting for a touch of care

THE LADDER OF LIFE

The ladder of life
Majority have been on this ladder
And most of us are still here

How do you weigh the energy required to climb this ladder?
This ladder is for the mind on a mission
This is a ladder of uncertainties

This ladder is a channel to reach the top
The beginning of every journey is easy
What happens when you get tired?

The toughest stage is when you find yourself in crisis
This is not the time to give up on your journey
Conscious effort to push through difficult situation is key

Remember why you stepped on the ladder the first time
Rest when everything is on the low but don't give up
Harness all you've got and let the ladder serve your purpose

SOMETHING CALLED TIME

Time is perishable
As the clock ticks it can't be retrieved
Seasons are a continuous phenomenon

'Time is money' our elders said
There is time for everything, they added
Yet none made meaning until now

Time and seasons come and go
How they will turn out, no one knows
Time gives us the surprise of our lives

Each is unique and teaches us immensely
We either get caught up in good moments and hope they remain
Experience an unwanted situation and wish it was a dream

Time alone gives us meaning to life
Whether good or bad, none really lasts
Time tells, your time will come!

TIME AND TIDE

I have been there
And I'm sure you too have

Times are really hard
Life has become difficult

Relationships giving cold returns
Good friends are like diamonds in the sand

It has come to that time where all efforts welcome no pleasantry
Your sweat is seen as water from the laundry

You get to a point where you cannot fake smiles
Every minute of your life is being judged

We were supposed to be each other's keeper
What went wrong?

Yes, I have been there
A season can sprout that dry seed

Wipe your tears
Blow your nose

Make the Bible your friend
With Jesus in the boat, we will smile at the storm.

REMIND ME

Remind me of the good old days
The time we had no responsibilities
Those free moments we had nothing to think about

Remind me of our early years full of bliss
Where all we did was eat and play
No assignments nor life to plan

Remind me of the times we could be ourselves
Without anyone judging us
A life worth living

Remind me of all the things we aspired to be
Which made us eager to become adults
Forgetting nothing comes on a silver platter

Remind me of the good moments
Where everyone loved and cared
Remind me and take me back.

ENVY NO ONE

Envy no one
You have no idea the cross people carry
We were all born differently
Even twins do vary

We easily get misled by others
It's either we're disrupted or manipulated
Waste no time trying to figure someone out
Rather focus on yourself

Invest in yourself
Do things that make you happy
Engage in activities to uplift your spirit
Make your world meaningful

Time is money
And time utilized well bring riches
Be purpose driven
Time wasted can never be regained

The difference is the purpose with which we operate
Tune your attention to yourself and make a difference
Do not be influenced by another's lifestyle
Own your life and your world.

PAIN AND PEOPLE

Pain affects people in diverse ways
We all have different thresholds of pain
What you may endure may affect another

Everyone is entitled to life and a chance to live
Life isn't exciting when you're alone
This makes human association inevitable

Relationships become a necessity
We invite others to share life with
Making us vulnerable and victims of undesirable behaviours

Pain has adverse effects on people
Most people have their mental health compromised
Worse experiences affect future relationships

Pain should not be part of life
When you inflict any form of pain on another
Prepare for the consequences of your actions as pain
changes people.

'NO' IS A RESPONSE

No is a response
Such a simple word
Yet a strong reply

Don't feel obliged to always say yes to people's requests
Some people disregard others plight and expect a yes
No is a response and this should be normalised

We have been made uncomfortable by the word no
Psych yourself to accept undesirable response as an individual
Situations will not always turn in your favour

It's obvious we aren't used to negative feedback
Let's turn undesirable response as a reinforcement than a setback
No is a response, embrace it.

SELF-CONFIDENCE

Confidence is the spice to life
Whereas self-confidence serves as an ingredient to your personality
Among all other personality traits confidence is unmatched

Confidence is the new currency to life
Self-confidence has been misunderstood and misinterpreted as arrogance
Many families fail to nurture this rare personality in their wards

Timidity was the gold of old
Confidence was rather sabotaged
These bunch of gold are now stuck due to their shy nature

Wake up and flow with time
No need to sabotage confident people
They are the future we need

Great leaders don't just emerge
Good qualities groom exceptional leaders
Let's encourage self-confidence.

STAY FOCUSED

It is impossible to maintain one's focus in this chaotic world
A century packed with wavering situations confusing our generation
Stand aloof and become victim of circumstances

Gone are the days where there was freedom of movement
Now the introduction of many viruses has crippled mankind
And the fear of the unknown has killed personal growth

What more can we do aside from our daily routines?
External forces draw us back
Diverse opinions cloud our minds and confuse our decisions

Is there any easy way out?
Even though nothing comes easy
Let's discover some ways to staying tune

Make use of timelines
Focus on things you love doing
Centralize on your motivation.

WE ARE UNIQUE

Everyone is unique in nature
There isn't an odd human
So don't compare yourself with anyone

Accept who you are
Discover your potentials
Watch your uniqueness raise eyebrows

We all cannot be the same
Why even body shame
Accept the difference

We are from various families
We possess different genes
It is impossible to look same

Some see diversity as flaws
Others call it character
I say we are unique

Creation would be meaningless
When we all look alike
Embrace diversity

BE ENCOURAGED

We all have a place in this life
Don't be intimidated by anyone
Our journeys are diverse

Live your best days while you still can
Whatever is rightfully yours will be
Believe it won't go to anyone

If by any instance you lose anything to anyone
Do not lose yourself
You are all you've got

A loss or defeat in a situation is just the end of that chapter
and not your life
Accept it as a challenge and work on something new
You never know what the next chapter of your life has in
store for you

Give life a second chance when things don't seem to work
out
Develop a positive perception towards life
Your success will be evident when the time comes

WHEN ONE DOOR CLOSES

when one door closes another door opens
You've all come across this phrase
Why then should you be disappointed at a loss of an opportunity?

You forget this and cling onto the loss
You waste time grieving
You get drained of vital energy behind closed doors

Why lament over a decision that has been finalized?
Know your worth
Prepare for change

The world is pregnant with opportunities
Settle where you are valued
Only then will you enjoy life

Look around for breakthroughs when one door closes
Face the world with confidence
Utilise the many doors waiting to welcome you.

DECIDE TO SURVIVE

Life is a gift
Just like any other gift
Life is supposed to be pleasant

Sadly, we had awful journeys
Paths that were slippery and too steep
We were chased with arrows of betrayal and rejection

Places we searched for comfort rather drained our energy
The world seemed to be full of wrong people
Envious pals and spiteful colleagues

Anyone could have given up
why are some people mean?
Those who have all the time to destroy others

Life is full of ups and downs
Learn through every step of the way
Bad days are tests

Strength comes from the Lord
He continues to watch over His own
Trust in the Lord

You are all you've got
Don't give up
After every dark night comes a bright shining day

Bless God our past don't define us
He blesses and restores in His time
Decide to survive.